Revelation 1: 1-3

Spirit of Prophecy Bible Study

By Kurt E. Klopfenstein

Revelation 1: 1-3

Spirit of Prophecy

Bible Study

For precept must be upon precept,

precept upon precept;

line upon line,

line upon line; here a little, and there a little.

(ISAIAH 28:10)

CONTENTS

Authors Testimony

Greetings. My prayer is that as you go through this book, you will pray and ask for guidance from God's Holy Spirit, so He can teach you His ways.

When I was growing up, I only went to church on Easter and Christmas. To be honest, I didn't even think about God until I met my wife, Pam. She attended a Missionary Baptist Church, so when she invited me to go with her, I wasn't worried about going, in fact, I wanted to go, because I knew something was missing in my life and I needed to find out what it was.

For several services, I heard the pastor deliver his sermons. I observed many people going to the altar to pray when the invitation was given, but I didn't know why they went forward. Some said they needed God to restore the joy of their salvation; others testified about how the Lord saved them. I began to question these things. *What do these people have that I don't? How can I get it?* I even witnessed a little boy going forth to pray; then testifying about how God saved his soul. He was twelve-years old. I thought if he could understand then why can't I?

One Sunday morning, I listened intently to every word the pastor said. After he delivered his sermon, and while he was giving the altar call, I felt like I was standing *alone* in a crowd of about three-hundred people. To be honest, it felt as if an *earthquake* was going on inside of me. I felt bad, because I knew I was a sinner in need of salvation. I knew the only way I could obtain what was missing in my life was to surrender to the invitation God's Holy Spirit was giving me. No one else could do it for me. This was a journey only I could pursue. Every word the pastor said as he came down the aisle, still preaching, penetrated my soul. I didn't have to ask anyone who was speaking to my heart, because I already knew it was the Holy Spirit. I was hearing a voice inside that I had never heard before, telling me He loved me. In essence, Jesus Christ, *revealed* himself to me that day, and I needed Him to save my soul from hell. But then along came Satan. He told me, "You don't need this. This isn't for you. There'll always be another time." The Holy Spirit being the "Good Guy" wanted me to open my heart's door and just believe that Jesus died for my sins. But Satan, "The Evil Guy" was doing his best to talk me out of it. What I found amazing was this: God gave me the strength to go forward and pray and gave me the strength to believe. As the church sang *Just as I am,* I took the first step of faith in my *heart* by believing Jesus died for my sins on an old rugged cross. The Lord saved my soul that day and the heaviness I had in my heart was lifted. In return, I got joy unspeakable and full of glory. I later learned, I could have knelt in my pew to pray, or I could have just prayed in my seat. I have heard people testify about how they were saved in their bedroom at home, and others said they were saved when they were driving their car down the road. I have witnessed my own children get saved. What is important is that when the Holy Spirit gives the invitation, then that is the time to heed to His call. This isn't a head decision; it's a heart decision. I'm thankful I heeded to His invitation.

It is my prayer that when the Holy Spirit bids you to come, that you'll heed to His invitation too.

Your friend,

Kurt E. Klopfenstein

Reading and Understanding

A few years after the Lord had saved me, I decided it was time to read the Bible from the beginning to the end. So night after night, while I was at work, and when time allowed, I began my journey through the Bible. Almost a year later, I had learned about the twelve tribes of Israel, I read about battles they encountered, and I tried to focus in on what the children of Israel did that was in opposition to God. But if someone asked me a question about the Bible, I found it hard to explain. Now I know why I could not explain it: simply because the Bible has too much information to absorb in a year.

One night, I joined in on a Bible study at our church. We were studying out of the books of Leviticus and Exodus. A year later, we had studied roughly five chapters. It was then I began to understand what Isaiah the prophet meant in Isaiah 28:10. My pastor did not have to tell me what Isaiah meant, because it was obvious. I had read the Bible from Genesis to Revelation, but I didn't have an understanding of much of what I had read. Like Isaiah said it's precept upon precept, line upon line, here a little, there a little. For me, this meant taking in smaller segments, meditating on them, and allowing the Holy Spirit to guide me on what it means, and what He wanted me to know. I came to realize that all the Scriptures point to Christ. The Old Testament has stories, which are a shadow, or a picture of things to come in the New Testament. And no matter what I had read, I could always find myself in the Scripture, meaning, the people in the Bible went through things I've gone through spiritually. We're given treasures in the Word if we search the Scripture with a *spiritual* understanding and not a *carnal* mind. I can honestly say, I could spend the rest of my life studying the Bible and still not understand it all, because it is given in bits and pieces; here a little, and there a little, but it will all line up and point to Jesus Christ. He is the center of it. Sometimes I get stuck when reading a passage of Scripture, but I have found that if I pray and meditate on it long enough, then when the Holy Spirit wants me to know what it means, He will show me, because it takes God to reveal the Scriptures. When He does show me, it blesses my soul.

A preacher once said that in order to understand the book of Revelation, we must realize that there is an inner and an outer man, meaning there are two of us. I like what Paul said in Romans 7: 22. *For I delight in the law of God after the inward man.* (V.25) *I thank God through Jesus Christ, our Lord. So then with the mind I myself serve the law of God, but with the flesh the law of sin.* Since I've accepted the Lord into my heart, I know my spirit is willing to do what is right when it comes to serving the Lord, but my flesh is weak. I have to keep my flesh under subjection, and make the flesh obey, so that I can be a light to the world. But when I do sin, I ask God to forgive me, because I want others to see Christ living in me. But I also know that God did not save my flesh when I got saved; he saved my soul. *Because the carnal mind is enmity against God: for it is not subject to the law of God, neither can it be.* (Romans 8: 7). *So then they that are in the flesh cannot please God. But ye are not in the flesh, but in the Spirit, if so be that the Spirit of God dwell in you. Now if any man have not the Spirit of Christ, he is none of you.* (Romans 8: 8-9). It took me awhile to understand this, but once I did, I realized it's my inner being, my soul, that God saved. And he's keeping it forever. *Whosoever is born of God **doth not** commit sin; for his seed remaineth in him: and he **cannot sin**, because he is born of God.* (I John 3:9). I had a little trouble understanding what God meant by this, because I know I will always sin in the flesh, but God meant something spiritual. He saved my soul, so I became a of born again child of God, and the seed in me is Christ, and since Christ can't sin, neither can I in my soul. But as long as I have the outer man, in my flesh I will continue to sin, because God didn't save my flesh, but my soul. Once I understood this, I was able to study the Book of Revelation with a much better understanding of how God looks at things. He does so with a spiritual mind.

And except those days should be shortened, there should no flesh be saved: but for the elect's sake those days shall be shortened. (Matthew 24: 22). I wondered why He said that did no "flesh" would be saved ? Because when we sin, we sin in the *flesh* and *not* in the soul. God tells us no one is righteous. *For Christ also hath once suffered for sins, the just for the unjust, that he might bring us to God, being put to death in the flesh, but quickened by the Spirit:* (I Peter 3:18). God is telling us that His only Begotten Son, Jesus, was the just person who died for the unjust so that He might bring us to God. Jesus came to earth in the flesh, bore our sins upon Him, died, and God raised Jesus from the dead, because there was no sin in Him. So when we truly get saved and accept Christ as our savior, we are buried in his death, burial, and resurrection, and we're raised up with Him in newness of life. *The like figure whereunto even baptism (not putting away of the filth of the flesh, but the answer of a good conscience toward God,) by the resurrection of Jesus Christ.* (I Peter 3;21). Whenever I ponder on this Scripture, my mind always goes back to the thief on the cross. He believed Jesus was dying for him, and Jesus told him that starting that day, he'd be with Him forever in paradise. The thief did not come down off the cross to be baptized in water. He just believed that Jesus was dying for his sins. So this affirmed with me that water baptism could not help me get to heaven. I had to have a spiritual baptism like the thief on the cross. And this took place in my soul the day I too believed Christ died for my sins. Every individual has to have a good conscience toward God by believing His Son, Jesus, died for their sins and that God raised Jesus from the dead. *And they said, Believe on the Lord Jesus Christ, and thou shalt be saved, and thy house.* (Acts 16:31). Now since I'm saved, I can say that I am *righteous*, not in my outer man, my flesh, but in my soul. And that's only because I took Christ as my personal savior, and He gave me a robe of righteousness. That same minute I trusted in Him for the saving of my soul, he baptized me into His death inwardly. A week after I was saved, our pastor baptized me in the church baptistery just to show what took place inwardly, but I also realized the water in the baptistery couldn't save me, just like the Bible says. It cannot wash away the sin I had in my soul. *I will greatly rejoice in the Lord; my soul shall be joyful in my God; for he hath clothed me with the garments of salvation, he hath covered me with the robe of righteousness, as a bridegroom decketh himself with ornaments, and as a bride adorneth herself with her jewels.* (Isaiah 61:10).

I love the song titled: *When He Sees Me.* The words in this song rang true for me. *When He sees me, He sees the blood of the Lamb. He sees me as worthy and not as I am.* I'm glad God made it that way. If I was counting on myself and my good works to make it to heaven, I'd fall short, because in my flesh, I cannot keep from sinning, because I am human. How dare I try to take any credit for what Jesus did for me at the cross, taking my sins upon Himself freely, and dying for them, so I could have access back to God. I cannot take any credit, because then I would be exalting myself above God, and telling myself it is by my works that justifies me, and not by what Jesus came to do at the cross. He did all of the work for me, and all I had, just like the thief on the cross was to believe.

Before we venture into Revelation, it's important to lay ground work so we can see a physical picture of spiritual things, so the next section focuses on this.

Foundation for Understanding

When I first began to study the book of Revelation, I thought it's too deep. Only bible scholars or preachers can figure out what God means, but the more I began to pray for guidance from the Holy Spirit, I found out I was able to understand, because I was not relying on myself. I enjoy studying what Christ already accomplished for me at the cross. And I'm happy that John shares his experience with us in Revelation, because he has the same testimony that I have. John was in the *spirit* and a witness to what he recorded in Revelation. Anyone who has been saved has the same testimony John has. So while studying, you can have the assurance that you too can understand the book of Revelation, because it is your experience as well.

It is also important to distinguish what prophecy means. God said for the testimony of Jesus is the spirit of prophecy. *And I, John, fell at his feet to worship him. And he said unto me, See thou do it not: I am thy fellow servant, and of thy brethren that have the testimony of Jesus, worship God: for the* **testimony of Jesus is the spirit of prophecy.** (Revelation 19:10). *Therefore the Lord himself shall give you a sign; Behold, a virgin shall conceive, and bear a son, and shall call his name Immanuel.* (Isaiah 7:14). Isaiah was simply telling us what was going to happen and it was fulfilled in Matthew. *Now the birth of Jesus Christ was on this wise: When as his mother Mary was espoused to Joseph, before they came together, she was found with child of the Holy Ghost. And knew her not till she had brought forth her firstborn son: and he called his name JESUS.* (Matthew 1:18; 25). I have the testimony of Jesus Christ in me. This happened to me the minute I got saved and took Christ as my personal savior. God inspired Adam in the garden when he breathed into Adam's nostrils the breath of life; and man became a living soul. (Genesis 2:7). *And so it is written. The first man Adam was made a living soul: the last Adam was made a quickening spirit.* (I Corinthians 15:45). I too was made a quickening spirit, because I have the testimony of Jesus in me. The truth is this: The whole Bible is about Jesus Christ and what He did for us at the cross.

For years, I have heard people refer to "Revelation" as "Revelations." The latter is not the case. "Revelations" means plural. "Revelation" is singular, meaning one—the revelation of Jesus Christ; when He **reveals** Himself to us as an individual. He reveals Himself to us by His Spirit. When the Lord revealed Himself to me, I didn't have to turn and ask my wife who was speaking to my heart. I knew it was the Holy Spirit, and I knew Jesus died for my sins. But before I could be saved, I had to recognize that I was a sinner in need of salvation. When did this happen? The day I came to the knowledge of good and evil, the day my conscience bothered me and let me know when I did something wrong. Just like the two thieves on the cross. One thought he didn't do anything wrong, but the other thief realized he had and that he needed Jesus to save him. That same thing had happened to me. I knew I was lost and without hope, and dead in my trespasses of sin. In the Garden, Adam and Eve knew they had sinned, too. But the good news is this: once I heard the gospel, glad tidings, I knew I could be forgiven of my sins by believing Jesus already paid the cost. The most important thing to remember is this: sin brings death to us all, but the gospel brings life through Jesus Christ our Lord.

Even Noah had the same faith that I have even though Jesus had not come to the earth yet to pay for Noah's sins, but yet, it was as if Jesus had already done it. We find evidence of this in Revelation 5:6. What John saw: *And I beheld, and, lo, in the midst of the throne and of the four beasts, and in the midst of the elders, stood a Lamb as it had been slain, having seven horns and seven eyes, which are the seven Spirits of God sent forth into all the earth.* John wept because no man in heaven, nor in earth, neither under the earth, was able to open the book, neither to look thereon. The Bible says, John wept much because no one was found worthy. But one of the elders said to John, "Weep not: behold, the Lion of the tribe of Judah, The Root of David, hath prevailed to open the book, and to loose the seven seals thereof." Therefore, we see evidence that before the world was, Jesus was going to pay our sin debt. Job understood this too even though the Bible had not been in print yet. *For I know that my redeemer liveth, and that he shall stand at the latter day upon the earth.* (Job 19: 25). Job understood that Jesus Christ was going to be his redeemer, and the redeemer for everyone who believes.

God knew we were all going to sin and need a redeemer, someone who could rescue us, and make a way for us to be restored back to Him. He knew that Adam and Eve were going to sin in the Garden. *And the Lord God commanded the man, saying, of every tree of the garden thou mayest freely eat: But of the tree of the knowledge of good and evil, though shalt not eat of it; for in the day that thou eatest thereof thou shalt surely die.* (Genesis 2:16-17). Therefore, we know that God already had a plan to take care of Adam and Eve's sin, because in the midst of the Garden, He also had the Tree of Life, which is Christ. Adam and Eve didn't die a physical death that day, but rather a spiritual death. Simply put, sin had slew them, and the only way they could be restored back to God was if they took of the Tree of Life, which is Christ, by believing Jesus, the Lamb slain before the foundation of the world was going to come and pay their sin debt, because He is our redeemer. Today we have to believe the same thing. We also learn that Noah found grace in the eyes of the Lord. (Genesis 6:8). And so did Abraham. *What shall we say then that Abraham our father, as pertaining to the flesh hath found? For if Abraham were justified by his works, he hath whereof to glory; but not before God. For what saith the scripture? Abraham believed God, and it was counted unto him for righteousness.* (Romans 4: 1-3). So we learn that even Abraham couldn't do anything in the flesh to justify his works in the flesh. He just simply *believed God*. If we allow ourselves to meditate on the fact that Abraham believed God, and God counted that to him as righteousness, it becomes clear to us just how simple it really is to be saved, and to be kept by God. The writer is telling us that what we needed to make us a child of God was performed by the Lord Jesus at the cross, and our job is just to *believe* it, like Abraham did.

The day I got saved, God gave me the power to become a son of God. I couldn't start from the point where I got saved and then try to work my way into heaven. I don't dare take credit for anything that Jesus accomplished for me at the cross. Because I am a man, and I will continue to sin in the flesh as long as I'm in this world. The power was given to me the moment I received Christ as my personal savior—I became a son of God. *The Spirit itself beareth witness with our spirit, that we are the children of God: And if children, then heirs; heirs of God, and joint-heirs with Christ.; if so be that we suffer with him, that we may be glorified together.* (Romans 8: 16-17). So that puts the big *I's* and the little *u's* out of the equation.

I've talked to many people who say they don't understand the Bible, and to be honest, they seemed bored with church. It takes dedication when you're studying the Word, and meditation, as I have found. When those two things are factored in, it's not boring because the Holy Spirit stands ready to show us something new in the Word we haven't seen before. But if you don't read it, He can't teach you. One time I had bought an entertainment center. I laid out all the pieces. Two hours later, I was still sitting there, scratching my head, wondering why I could not figure out how to put it together. My wife came to me and asked if I had read the instructions. She told me the manufacturer put the instructions in the box for a reason. I continued to put it together, still not taking her advice. By the time I finished, I had extra parts that I threw away. But her statement caused me to apply this to the Word of God. He gave us instructions to read it and let it sink in. The same thing happened to me when I bought my boat. One day I could not figure out how to take off the oil filter, because I had not read the book. Later that day, I took my boat to a dealer who fixed it for me. After a costly repair, I decided it was time for me to learn how to do things on my own. The same principle applies when studying the Word of God. If we don't study, He can't teach us anything.

My fellow coworkers question me at times about what church or religion in which I am affiliated. I tell them I am a Baptist and that I am saved and going to heaven. I also like to mention the fact that anyone who is saved by God is a member of the church above, New Jerusalem. God doesn't divide us. We are all in one family, the family of God, if we have been saved. I have also been asked which religion is the right one. To which I respond, "It's not about religion. It is about salvation. If you are going to a church that teaches and preaches that Jesus died for our sins, and that God raised Him from the dead, and you can feel the Holy Spirit when you go to church, and you're witnessing people getting saved, then you're going to a good church." It's not about what church you go to as long as the church puts Jesus at the center of it all, because it's so important to remember who we were before we got saved and who we are now—born again children of God. He needs us to study and pray and go to church so we can be a witness to others. The more I study my Bible; it thrills my soul every time the Lord shows me something I haven't seen before. I'm like John when he leapt in his mother's womb. Mary went to visit Elizabeth after she'd been with child six months. And when Elizabeth heard the salutation of Mary, the Bible says that John leapt. He did so because the spirit moved. The same is true with me, whenever I hear the Spirit, not with my ears, but with my soul, my soul leaps within me. I appreciate those times. It's what I long for. And it's what the writers in the Bible, given by the inspiration of the Holy Spirit were talking about. If we're saved, we're not waiting to go into Zion, because anytime we operate in the Spirit, and feel the Lord, we're in Zion. I don't have to be in church to operate in the Spirit, although I love worshipping with my brothers and sisters in Christ, but there have been times I've been driving to work, and listening to a recorded church service on a CD, and the Lord will bless me to feel His Spirit. There are times, I want to feel His Spirit, but I cannot. It's all in God's timing. I come to learn that God is not in the time zone we are in. He has His own timing, and it's perfect. Every time.

Even the law of God is not based on time. It's not something that's given for this brief amount of time on this earth, but rather, it's eternal. God has given a law that He himself is held to, and so are we. God told Adam, I forbid you to eat of the tree of knowledge of good and evil, for the day you eat of it, ye shall surely die, so it's a truth—God kept his promise. Once we realize we are a sinner, we too ate of that tree of knowledge of good and evil, just like Adam and Eve, and our eyes are opened to the fact that we are lost and undone without God, and need a covering for our sin, because we are naked. That covering for our sins is Jesus Christ. He clothes us with a robe of righteousness. So we know our sins, and Adam and Eve's sins had to be dealt with. I wondered once why God couldn't just forgive me of my sin, because He knew what I was, but God couldn't lower His standard. *Therefore*—means because of what we learned prior—*all things whatsoever ye would that men should do to you, do ye even so to them: for this is the law and the prophets.* (Matthew 7:12). This is how heaven operates. In order to abide in heaven, then the law cannot be destroyed, one jot, nor one tittle. You cannot leave one little element out of it. That's why I found myself in a mess when it came to trying to keep the law, the Ten Commandments. When John was looking into eternal things in Revelation, he wasn't looking at things to come out in the near future; he was looking into the glory of heaven itself. And there was one that sat on the throne, having a book in his hand that was written within, and the backside, sealed with seven seals. That book was sealed up, and could not be opened. No one was found worthy to open it, neither in heaven nor in the earth, nor under the earth, that was worthy to take the book and loose the seals and to look thereon. You had to walk through the book to be on the backside of the book. If you study Genesis and Revelation, you will find the Tree of Life, Christ, in the beginning and He's the ending. But the Bible says that John wept. And one came to him and told him to weep not because there is one who has prevailed, there is one who is worthy to take the book and loose the seals. And in the midst, the tribe of Judea hath prevailed. The Lord came to the earth and took on the nature of man as a lion and an ox. The Lord being the

King of Kings came as a beast of burden into this world to bear the load of our sins upon him to the cross, so then he had the power to loose the seals of the book, so we could have access to God. We are unworthy of life, but through Jesus Christ our Lord, we can have life, if we believe in His work he performed at the cross, then we get everything we need to be saved. The Lord came and revealed those things which are unseen. There's more to the cross then what meets the eye; more than we could ever imagine.

Listen to what Jeremiah the prophet wrote. *Is there no balm in Gilead, is there no physician there? Why then is not the health of the daughter of my people recovered?* (Jeremiah 8:22). The answer is yes, there is balm in Gilead. Jesus Christ came to pay our sin debt, so our sin-sick soul could be healed. *And he said, Go, and tell this people, Hear ye indeed, but understand not; and see ye indeed, but perceive not. Make the heart of this people fat, and make their ears heavy, and shut their eyes; lest they see with their eyes, and hear with their ears, and understand with their heart, and convert, and be healed.* (Isaiah 6:6-9). The day we get saved, we are converted, and we have a healing for our sin-sick soul. Christ is the balm; He's the great physician, He's the healer.

When Jesus was on the cross and He cried out "My God, My God. Why hast thou forsaken me?" Jesus allowed himself to come down to the place where I was to be numbered among the transgressors, to be counted as one of the sinners, as though he had sinned, but yet, he had no sin in Him. He took my sin on Him. And if I was the only who He would've needed to die for, He would've done it, because He loves me that much. When John wept, and was told not to weep because there was one worthy to open the seals of the book, it was meaning that Christ would be the one to loose the seals, do everything that was needed at the cross, so that you and I, and John, and all nations could be saved. What Christ did at the cross for us, is more powerful then sin itself. It's more powerful than the power of hell or death, *our two enemies,* because a righteous man, came to die for us. This is the fulfillment of the law and the prophets. If the law itself was good enough to get me to heaven, then Christ would've never had to come to pay my sin debt. Many people don't take into consideration there is more to the law then just the Ten Commandments. The law of righteousness contains another law that a lot of people leave out, and that is the law of charity—doing for others for what they cannot do for themselves—where a just man would die for the unjust man. Christ did for us what we couldn't do for ourselves. And that's the fulfillment of the law that Christ kept. He fulfilled the law and the only thing we have to do is believe. John knew he was in a fix too, that's why he was weeping, but then he spiritually saw the Lamb, Christ, slain before the foundation of the world, and John knew that Jesus Christ had done it for him.

Did Christ come to do away with the law? Absolutely not. He came to fulfill it, because He was the only one *righteous* enough to do it for us. That's why I said I can take no credit for my salvation, or anything that Christ did for me. *Think not that I am come to destroy the law, or prophets: I am not come to destroy but to fulfill.* (Matthew 5:17). Jesus was saying the law cannot be destroyed; only that He is fulfilling it. He already did. All we have to do is *believe* like Noah and Abraham, so that God can count that to us as righteousness. People on the earth address me as "Kurt Klopfenstein" but inwardly, the day the Lord saved my soul, like Jacob in the Old Testament, I got a new name. My spiritual name is Kurt Israel, and I'm dwelling in the land of Beulah. *Thou shalt no more be termed Forsaken; neither shall thy land any more be termed Desolate: but thou shalt be called Hephzibah, and thy land Beulah: for the Lord delighteth in thee, and thy land shall be married.* (Isaiah 62:4). Jesus Christ had already paid His vows to me, and the day I stood before the church and testified that I had accepted Christ as my personal savior, I paid my wedding vows to Him, and now I'm dwelling with him in The Land of Beulah, the married land. This means I'm joined with Christ. He's never letting go of me, and I can't let go of Him. Where He is, I am. God promised me that.

All the Lord ever asked of us was to believe Him. In the mind of God, Jesus had already paid our sin debt because John seen him in the spirit and what he'd done when he said, he'd seen a lamb that had been slain before the foundation of the world, that means, before the earth or anything existed. John looked and he saw Him right in the midst of all of us, because Christ is the center of it all. He is the Scripture. It's all Him.

In the next section, we will look at Revelation 1:1, and break it down, so you too can have a better understanding. But we have to take into consideration what Isaiah said in regard to line upon line, precept upon precept, here a little and there a little, so I've interwoven stories and other Scriptures to give a picture of something spiritual. God did not intend for his Word to scare people of future things to come. The only thing we need to fear is going to hell like the rich man. Hell is as real as heaven. I'm so glad I made the choice to go to heaven. You can too.

Revelation 1: 1

The Revelation of Jesus Christ, which God gave unto him, to shew unto his servants things which must shortly come to pass; and he sent and signified it by his angel unto his servant John. (1:1).

*Now to him that is of power to stablish you according to my gospel, and the preaching of Jesus Christ, according to the revelation of the mystery, which was kept secret since the world began. But now is made manifest, and by the scriptures of the prophets, according to the commandment of the everlasting God, made known to all nations for the **obedience of faith**.* (Romans 16:25-26).

*For God so loved the world, that he gave his only begotten Son, that whosoever believeth in him should not perish, but have **everlasting life**. For God sent not his Son into the world to **condemn** the world; **but that the world through Him might be saved.*** (John 3: 16-17).

Early tradition says that John was banished to Patmos by the Roman authorities. *I John, who also am your brother, and companion in tribulation, and in the kingdom and patience of Jesus Christ, was in the isle of Patmos, for the word of God, and for the testimony of Jesus Christ.* (V: 9). I compare my spiritual walk with the Lord to John. He was on the isle of Patmos, for the word of God, and for the testimony of Jesus Christ, just like I live in Huber Heights Ohio, for the word of God, and for the testimony of Jesus Christ. If you've been saved by God, than you too have the testimony of Jesus Christ in you. *I was in the Spirit on the Lord's day, and heard behind me a great voice, as of a trumpet.* (1:10). I think it's important to note that John was in the Spirit.

It amazes me when little children get saved. They understand that Jesus Christ **revealed** himself unto them. And because they are young, they may not understand much about the Word, but they can tell you they invited Jesus into their hearts, and they can tell you the day *Jesus Christ* revealed himself unto them. I didn't understand the things that happened to me when I got saved, but I did know that I had heard the Word preached, and I knew I was under conviction, and that the Holy Spirit was giving me the invitation to be saved, just like all the little children I've witnessed being saved. All I had to do was to repent and believe. That same day the Spirit was knocking at my heart's door, Jesus *revealed* himself to me. So when we look at the Book of Revelation, we have to understand that John is telling his experience, just like we tell our experience. If we're saved, we all have an experience to share about the *day* the Lord saved our soul from hell.

I remember a Bible story I once read about the wise men found in Matthew 2: 1-14. I love this story because it shows how wise men made their journey to where Jesus was born. The wise men came from the east to Jerusalem, because they saw the star in the east, and they wanted to worship the baby being born who would be King of the Jews.

I can relate to the wise men, because when I began going to church with my wife, I had a longing in my soul. I knew I needed Jesus. I kept going to church, because I knew that eventually Jesus would save me. So in essence, I was wise, just like the wise men, because I too had a journey to make to come to the Lord.

But when King Herod had heard these things he was troubled, and all of Jerusalem was too, and he called for the chief priest and scribes, and demanded of them where Christ should be born. *And they said unto him, In Bethlehem, in the land of Judea: for thus it is written by the prophet.* (2:5). *But thou, Bethlehem Ephratah, though thou be little among the thousands of Judah, yet out of thee shall he come forth unto me that is to be ruler in Israel; whose goings forth have been from of old, from everlasting.* (Micah 5:2). *And thou Bethlehem, in the land of Judea, art not the least among the princes of Judea: for out of thee shall come a Governor, that shall rule my people Israel.* (Matthew 2: 6).

Shortly thereafter, when King Herod had heard these things, he called for the wise men, and asked them what time the star appeared. Then the king told them to go and seek diligently for the young child, and when they found him, to bring him word again, so that he could go and worship him too. But the truth is, King Herod wasn't going to go worship Jesus, he planned to kill Him. *And when they were departed, behold, the angel of the Lord appeareth to Joseph in a dream saying, Arise, and take the young child and his mother, and flee into Egypt, and be thou, there until I bring thee word: for Herod will seek the young child to destroy him.* (Matthew 2: 13).

This reminds me of my journey to the Lord. I was standing in the church, listening to the preacher deliver his sermon. Then while the choir was singing, the Holy Spirit was giving me the invitation to come and accept Christ as my savior, but Satan was trying to deceive me, just like King Herod was trying to deceive the wise men.

But what King Herod didn't understand was this: Jesus didn't plan to take his earthly throne from him. Jesus came to earth and He died, to be the Governor of spiritual Israel. *For unto us a child is born, unto us a son is given: and the government shall be upon his shoulder: and his name shall be called Wonderful, Counsellor, The mighty God, The everlasting Father, The Prince of Peace. Of the increase of his government and peace there shall be no end, upon the throne of David, and upon his kingdom, to order it, and to establish it with judgement, and with justice from henceforth even for ever. The zeal of the Lord of hosts will perform this.* (Isaiah 9:6-7).

And thou Bethlehem, in the land of Judea, art not the least among the princes of Judea: for out of thee shall come a Governor that shall rule my people Israel. (Matthew 2: 6). When I got saved, I got adopted into spiritual Israel. *But Jerusalem which is above is free, which is the mother of us all.* (Galatians 4:26). I'm freed from sin, no longer held captive to it, and my heavenly mother is Jerusalem. It's the church.

And Jacob was left alone; and there wrestled a man with him until the breaking of the day. And when he saw that he prevailed not against him, he touched the hollow of Jacob's thigh; and the hollow of Jacob's thigh was out of joint, as he wrestled with him. And he said, Let me go, for the day breaketh. And he said, I will not let thee go, except thou bless me. And he said, Thy name shall be called no more Jacob, but Israel: for as a prince hast thou power with God and with men, and hast prevailed. (Genesis 22: 24-28). *And Jacob called the name of the place Peniel: for I have seen God face to face, and my life is preserved.*

This is what happened to me when I got saved. God preserved my life. I am no longer dead in my trespasses of sin, living in the land of the dead, but rather I'm in the land of the living. And just like John, and all the other prophets, and all of my other brothers and sisters in Christ, I'm now under a new government, and I'm part of a kingdom that will be everlasting. *Therefore the children of Israel eat not of the sinew which shrank, which is upon the hollow of the thigh, unto this day: because he touched the hollow of Jacob's thigh in the sinew that shrank.* This happened to me too. When the Lord saved my soul that day, I put on Christ and now I walk different, because I'm a born again child of God, meaning, there was a change in my soul, and it's the desire of my heart, to let my inner change show outwardly.

Since I've been saved, the devil still gives me a hard time. He didn't have to before I was saved, because he already had me where he wanted me. Even being saved I've had times where I questioned if what I have is real? But then I remember I'm dealing with an inner and outer man. The outer man will always give us a hard time, but the more I study the Word, and go to church, and pray, I feel the Holy Spirit of God and He assures me it's real. I can honestly say that when I'm in a church service, and the Lord lays it on my heart to pray for someone, and then that someone gets saved, I receive a blessing of seeing them saved, because I prayed for them like God instructed me to do. So in the spirit, God allows us to know what's right. *But the natural man receiveth not the things of the Spirit of God: for they are foolishness unto him: neither can he know them, because they are spiritually discerned.* (I Corinthians 2:14).

So, *The Revelation of Jesus Christ, which God gave unto him, to shew unto his servants things which must shortly come to pass; and he sent and signified it by his angel unto his servant John:*

The "him" is Jesus. So the revelation of Jesus comes from God. To shew unto his servants things which must shortly come to pass. *At that time Jesus answered and said, I thank thee, O Father, Lord of heaven and earth, because thou hast hid these things from the wise and prudent, and hast revealed them unto babes. All things are delivered unto me of the Father: and no man knoweth the Son, but the Father, neither knoweth any man the Father, save the Son, and he to whomever the Son will **reveal** him. Come unto me, all ye that labour and are heavy laden, and I will give thee rest. For my yoke is easy, and my burden is light.* (Matthew 11: 25; 27; 28; 30). So we know that Jesus has the revelation and shows it to his servants. And He gives us rest once we get saved. *For I tell you, that many prophets and kings have desired to see these things which ye see, and have not seen them; and to hear those things which ye hear, and have not heard them.* (10:24). This shows me we cannot seek God by being book smart. It's a spiritual work. Once you get saved, you get the wisdom of God. There is not one unwise person in the family of God. What I mean by this is that some people may think themselves wise in all things, but they study God's word and try to interrupt it with a natural mind and cannot. God doesn't reveal it to the wise and prudent, meaning, we cannot dissect it ourselves and figure out what it means on our own. It takes God to reveal the Scriptures.

And the seventy returned again with joy, saying, Lord, even the devils are subject unto us through thy name. And he said unto them, I beheld Satan as lighting fall from heaven. Behold, I give unto you power to tread on serpents and scorpions, and over all the power of the enemy: and nothing shall by any means hurt you. Notwithstanding in this rejoice not, that the spirits are subject unto you; but rather rejoice, because your names are written in heaven.

Our pastor made reference one time to how it feels to be bitten by a mosquito. Before you realize you've been bitten, it's too late. It's already happened. That's how sin is. Once I realized I couldn't keep the law, I'd already failed. I was already dead in my trespasses of sin, and the only way I could get to God was to accept Christ as my savior. So like Paul, I was dead in my trespasses of sin, because sin slew me. *Oh wretched man that I am! Who shall deliver me from the body of this death? I thank God through Jesus Christ our Lord. So then with the mind I myself serve the law of God, but with the flesh the law of sin.* Sin stings is like the sting of a scorpion. I was dead in my trespasses of sin, but the gospel, glad tidings, gave me life. *What shall we say then? Is the law sin? God forbid. I had not known sin, but by the law; for I had not known lust, except the law had said, Thou shalt not covet. But sin, taking occasion by the commandment, wrought in me all manner of concupiscence. For without the law sin was dead. For I was alive without the law once; but when the commandment came, sin revived, and I died. And the commandment which was* **ordained to life, I found to be unto death**. *For sin, taking occasion by the commandment, deceived me, and by it slew me.* (Romans 7: 7-11). What Paul is teaching us is the fact that he thought the commandment was giving him life, but yet, when the commandment taught him he shouldn't covet, he'd already done it. And to him, this brought a spiritual death, because He couldn't keep the law. He knew he had to believe in the work Jesus did at the cross. Jesus was the only one who could keep the law. Anytime the Bible refers to ten horns, it's meaning the Ten Commandments, the law. As I mentioned before, Jesus came to earth, took on him the nature of flesh and was numbered as a transgressor, as though he had sinned, but yet He had no sin in Him. Jesus fulfilled the law from the age of 30 to 33 ½ years which is forty-two months, but He lived the law and did not sin, and had no sin in Him for 33 ½ years. He was the only one who could live it and not break one of the commandments. God was satisfied with the sacrifice and that's why He raised Jesus from the dead. Sin had to be paid for, and it was. And when Jesus walked the earth, He had every temptation that you and I could ever have, but He kept the law and fulfilled it.

When I think about what Jesus did, it makes me sad, but yet happy. It hurts me to know He had to die a horrible death for me, but yet I'm glad He did. If He had not done it, I would've never had the opportunity to be saved. None of us would.

I'll turn fifty this year. When I look back over my life, I think it really is just a vapor. I witnessed my four-year old, son, Jonathan, leave this world. It was heart-wrenching to see him go, but I know he's in heaven with our Lord, because he never came to the age of accountability. He was born with a ton of medical issues, and was mentally challenged, but thanks be to God, he takes innocent children home to heaven. Shortly after Jonathan died, many people asked me if I was mad at God. To be honest, I got on my knees after my son died and thanked God for allowing our family to have Jonathan for the short time we did. I wasn't mad at God. God doesn't send bad things our way. Sin does. I'm thankful the loving God we have takes little children home to heaven when they die, because He loves them. Jonathan was born into sin in the **flesh**, because we all inherit Adam's sin, but Jonathan's soul was in innocence. That's why he could go to heaven. You cannot be charged for something you know nothing about. Sin had not slain him yet. He didn't know the difference between right and wrong when he died, so he was safe with God. I have a lot of family members and friends who don't know Christ as their savior, and I want them to have what I have. Even though my son died a wrongful death, he's a lot better off than some of my family and friends, because at least Jonathan is with our Lord. I know, according to the Scripture, we only have a short time of span to see our people get saved. I want everyone I know, and the ones I don't know, to be saved, so that they too can have their place in heaven. So when I find myself weeping for my son, I have peace knowing I'll be reunited with him someday.

And he said unto me, Seal not the sayings of the prophecy of this book: for the time is at hand. (Revelation 22:10).

God is telling us not to seal up the testimony we was given when we accepted Jesus Christ as our savior, just like John didn't seal it up. In Revelation, John is sharing his experience with us. It's so important that we let our light shine to the world, so they too, can come to the saving knowledge of God.

For the time is at hand. I'm sitting here at my desk typing, and I see my tumbler filled with water, waiting for me to pick it up. The tumbler is within reach, just like time is at hand. When the Lord returns if you're not saved, you will spend eternity in hell. *He that is unjust, let him be unjust still; and he which is filthy, let him be filthy still; and he that is righteous, let him be righteous still; and he that is holy, let him be holy still.* (Revelation 22:11). This is talking about when Christ returns to get his bride—all born again believers who are wearing the robe of righteousness. If you're lost and undone and have never heeded to the call of the Holy Spirit, you will be unjust, but if you've been saved, you'll be righteous. I pray when He does return that you will be righteous.

And he sent and signified it by his angel unto his servant John. (1:1). Behold I come quickly: blessed is he that keepeth the sayings of the prophecy of this book. (Revelation 22:7). And I John saw these things, and heard them. And when I had heard and seen, I fell down to worship before the feet of the angel which shewed me these things. Then saith he unto me, See thou do it not; for I am thy fellowservant, and of thy brethren the prophets, and of them which keep the sayings of this book: worship God. (Revelation 22:8-9).

That's what God wants from us—for us to worship him in Spirit and in Truth. As Christians, we don't have the power to go in the name of the Lord if he's not moving us do to something, but if He is moving us to do something in His name, we should do it, because it's His angel moving us. But in order for his angel to move and bless us, we have to humble our hearts. And it's important we keep the sayings of the prophecy of this book—to tell others that Jesus saves.

On the next page, you will find a list of questions.

Reflection

Do you remember the day the Lord revealed Himself unto you? What do you remember?

_____

_____

_____

_____

_____

Why did John weep?

_____

_____

_____

_____

_____

Why did one of the elders tell John not to weep?

_____

_____

_____

_____

_____

Who was going to be the covering for Adam and Eve's sins?

_____
_____
_____
_____
_____

What is the law of charity?

_____
_____
_____
_____
_____

What is Grace?

_____
_____
_____
_____
_____

What made Abraham right with God?

_____
_____
_____
_____

What did Noah find in the eyes of the Lord? And why?

_____

_____

_____

_____

_____

Do you feel you have to work your way to heaven, or do you believe Christ did all of the work at the cross?

_____

_____

_____

_____

_____

What part of the man cannot sin? And why?

_____

_____

_____

_____

_____

Who was the Tree of Life in the Garden of Eden?

_____

_____

_____

_____

_____

Who was the only person found righteous enough to fulfill the law and why?

_____

_____

_____

_____

_____

Why did Jesus tell the thief on the cross that today he would be with Him in eternity?

_____

_____

_____

_____

_____

What is the definition of Prophecy?

_____

_____

_____

_____

_____

What is the definition of Revelation?

_____

_____

_____

_____

_____

Revelation 1: 2

John did pin this down. Everybody that's saved bears record of the word of God. Once we get saved, we get the record. It's in us. It's the testimony of Jesus Christ. *Who bare record of the word of God, and of the testimony of Jesus Christ, and of all things that he saw.* (Revelation 2:1).

If I take a Scripture in the Bible that don't mean anything to me, then it won't mean anything to you if I say it, so I have to have the record of Jesus in myself if I'm going to tell someone else about the Scripture. And when it's personal, and I say it and mean it, people will listen, because I'm telling my testimony, just like John is sharing his testimony with us.

Repent ye therefore, and be converted, that your sins may be blotted out, when the times of refreshing shall come from the presence of the Lord. (Acts 3:19). It's that simple. Just repent and believe when the Holy Spirit bids you to come, so you too can have a testimony.

John could only share with us what God showed him. And that's all we can do as Christians. If God hasn't revealed the Scriptures to us, we don't have any business trying to tell it wrong, or tell it like someone else told it, because the Spirit will not bless it, and in truth, I don't want to be guilty of telling lies on God, and neither should you. We shouldn't tell what we believe unless it's an absolute given by God.

Personal Testimony

Come and hear, all ye that fear God, and I will declare what he hath done for my soul. (Psalm 66:16). I love this testimony because David knew God saved his soul from hell.

My mouth shall shew forth thy righteousness and thy salvation all the day; for I know not the numbers thereof. (Psalm 71:15).

For we cannot but speak the things which we have seen and heard. (Acts 4:20). This is a truth.

We having the same spirit of faith, according as it is written, I believed, and therefore have I spoken; we also believe, and therefore speak. (II Corinthians 4:13). We're speaking of our testimony; the day the Lord saved our soul.

By Silvanus, a faithful brother unto you, as I suppose, I have written briefly, exhorting, and testifying that this is the true grace of God wherein ye stand. (I Peter 5:12).

The Woman with an Issue of Blood

Everyone who has been saved has a testimony and they are a witness of that day. In Mark 5: 25-34 this is about a woman who had heard Jesus was in the area and she had an issue of blood. When Jesus came by, she pressed from behind and touched His garment. She said, "If I may touch but his clothes, I shall be whole." The Bible says her blood was dried up. But once she touched His garment, she was **healed of her plaque**. Jesus immediately knew that virtue had gone out of him, and he asked, "Who touched my clothes?" He then looked around to see who had done this. And the woman fearing and trembling, knowing what was done in her body, came and fell down before Him, and told Him all truth. Christ said to her, "Daughter, thy *faith* hath made thee whole; go in peace, and be whole of thy *plaque.*"

We know Christ can do all things. He healed the sick, and performed many miracles. But this story has a deeper spiritual meaning too. Jesus Christ healed her sin-sick soul. She was plaqued with sin. Sin is what brings death to all of us. *Therefore shall her plaques come in one day, death and mourning, and famine; and she* *shall be utterly burned with fire: for strong is the Lord God who judgeth her. (Revelation 18:8). And I heard another voice from heaven, saying, Come out of her, my people, that ye be not partakers of her sins, and that ye receive not of her plaques. For her **sins** have reached unto heaven, and God hath remembered her inquities.* (Revelation 18:4-5).

In order for us to understand this, we must look at it with a spiritual mindset. *Her plaques shall come in one day, death and mourning, and famine; and she shall be utterly burned with fire; for strong is the Lord God who judgeth her. Come out of her my people, that ye be not partakers of her sins, and that ye receive not of her plaque. For her sins have reached unto heaven, and God hath remembered them.*

I'll use my four-year old son who passed as an illustration. When he passed, he had not come to the age of accountability where he knew right from wrong. And the Holy Spirit had not given him the invitation to accept Jesus Christ as his savior. So in essence, Jonathan went on to heaven, safe. Now me on the other hand, I too, was safe with God until the Holy Spirit gave me the invitation to come and be saved. That Sunday morning this happened to me, God remembered my sins. And I knew I was a sinner. I knew the difference between right and wrong. I was no longer safe because sin had slain me and I was dead in my trespasses of sin. The only way for me to get back to God, was to believe what the preacher preached—that Jesus came to pay for my sins so that I could go free. God said, "Come out of her my people, that ye be not partakers of her sins, and that ye receive not of her plaque. For her sins have reached unto heaven, and God hath remembered them." See God was telling me not only that I was a sinner, but I also had a way out. That even though I had eaten of the tree of knowledge of good and evil, realizing I was a sinner in need of salvation, and had the plaque of sin; He made a way for me to get out of the mess I was in. I only had to have the faith just like the woman with an issue of blood. Jesus told her that her faith hath made her whole and her plaque was removed. When I got saved, my plaque was removed and my sin-sick soul was healed. If you've been saved, yours was too.

Reflection

Who bares the record of the word of God?

_____

_____

_____

_____

_____

What must one do to be saved?

_____

_____

_____

_____

_____

When Jesus told the woman with an issue of blood that her faith
hath made her whole, what was the spiritual meaning of this
statement?

_____

_____

_____

_____

_____

What did God mean when He said: Come out of her my people, that ye be not partakers of her sins, and that ye receive not of her plaque?

_____

_____

_____

_____

_____

Who redeemed us from our sins?

_____

_____

_____

_____

_____

When do our sins come into God's remembrance?

_____

_____

_____

_____

_____

Revelation 1:3

Blessed is he that readeth, and they that hear the words of this prophecy, and keep those things which are written therein: for the time is at hand. (Revelation 1:3). *Behold I come quickly: blessed is he that keepeth the sayings of the prophecy of this book.* (Revelation 22:7). Blessed is happy. If we're going to learn anything from God, we have to study, not go on what everyone else says. We read, we hear, and understand, meaning keeping it close to our heart so we can tell others the hope that is within us, just like Peter said. Even Jesus' mother, Mary, pondered things in her heart.

In the previous sections, I shared several illustrations of how people came to the saving knowledge of God, and when Christ revealed himself to them. I also shared when Christ revealed Himself to me. But there is another story in the Bible that I love. It's the story of man named Nicodemus, a ruler of the Jews, and a Pharisee, who came to Jesus by night. (John 3: 1-21). I encourage you to read the story. In it, we know that Nicodemus recognized who Jesus was and knew of the miracles Jesus had performed. But Jesus said unto him, *"Verily, verily, I say unto thee, Except a man be born again, he cannot see the Kingdom of God. That which **is born of the flesh is flesh; and that which is born of the spirit is spirit.**"* Nicodemus no doubt was a good man, but Jesus told him he had to be born again. Jesus did not look at him and tell him he was good enough, or that he was right because he had religion, but rather He said, "Ye must be born again."

I love sharing how Jesus died on the cross for all of our sins. In Luke 23, we learned that people stood where Jesus was dying and they watched him die. One of the rulers said, "He saved others; let him save himself, if he be Christ, the chosen of God." And the soldiers mocked Him. They mistreated Jesus. They could not comprehend he was dying for them. A thief hung on each side of Jesus; two malefactors. One of them said to Jesus, "If thou be Christ, save thyself and us." But the other rebuked the other thief saying, "Dost not thou fear God, seeing thou art in the same condemnation? We receive the due rewards for our deeds; but this man hath done nothing amiss." This same thief that recognized he deserved death for what he had done, looked to Jesus and said, "Lord, remember me when thou comest into thy kingdom." And Jesus said unto him, "Verily I say unto thee, To day shalt thou be with me in paradise."

This story always brings tears to my eyes when I think about our Lord hanging between two thieves. One thief hanging there told Jesus "If thou be the Christ, save thyself and us." If that thief would have recognized that Jesus was dying for his sins, he too could have been saved like the other thief who trusted in the Lord that day. Jesus was dying for the sins of the whole world. We as individuals have to see what the Lord did for us at the cross if we too want to be saved, because we pierced him too. We were all guilty of putting him on the cross. He was dying for all of us. This is how simple salvation really is. The thief who trusted in Jesus to save him did not come off the cross and go into a body of water to be immersed. That which **is born of the flesh is flesh; and that which is born of the spirit is spirit.** Jesus baptized the soul of the thief who believed in him that day into His death, burial, and resurrection. The Bible tells us that blessed and holy is he that hath part in the first resurrection: on such, the second death hath no power, but they shall be priests of God and of Christ. The same day, the exact minute, the one thief took the Lord as his own personal savior and saw that Jesus was redeeming him from his sin, inherited eternal life in heaven, in paradise with our Lord forever. When the high priest washed in the brazen sea back in the Old Testament, this was a picture of being baptized in Christ resurrection. We go through the brazen sea when we get saved and he washes our sin sick soul

And death and hell were cast into the lake of fire. This is the second

death. And whosoever was not found written in the book of life was cast into the lake of fire. (Revelation 20: 14-15). The thief who believed died a physical death that day, but inwardly he died out to sin forever and took Jesus as his savior. But the other thief who didn't believe will spend eternity in hell.

And when the centurion, who stood there in front of Jesus, heard his cry and saw how Jesus died, he said, "Surely this man was the Son of God!" (Mark 15:39). The Roman at the cross was a Centurion, a Roman soldier. Because he is specifically called a centurion, he was more likely a higher ranking official in the Roman army, and had command of a group of soldiers. He is also mentioned in Matthew. *When the centurion, and they that were with him, watching Jesus, saw the earthquake, and those things that were done, they feared greatly, saying, "Truly this was the Son of God."* (Matthew 27:54). *Now when the centurion saw what was done, he glorified God, saying, "Certainly this was a righteous man."* (Luke 23:47). *But one of the soldiers with a spear, pierced his side, and forthwith came there out blood and water. And he that saw it* **bare record***, and his record is true, that he might believe.* (John 19: 34-35). The man who saw it has given his testimony, and his testimony is true. He knows that he tells the truth, and he testifies so that you also may believe. He bare the same record John had and tells about in Revelation.

I used the story of the thief one cross simply because I had read it and finally understood it with the help of the Lord. I understood I had to have the same faith as the thief, and I am blessed and I do have part in the first resurrection, and I'm thankful for that. It was all because of Jesus. I am also blessed when the Lord shows me something in the Bible I've never seen before. It thrills my soul. It is my desire to keep my flesh under subjection so I can help lead others to the Lord, because we only have a short time to see our people get saved.

If you read the Bible and have a hard time understanding it, I do hope you can understand what Jesus did for the thief on the cross, because He did the same thing for you, and all He is asking is that you have the same faith as the thief. A childlike faith. The faith of a grain of a mustard seed for the Lord to move that mountain of sin. It's that simple. I never want to portray my Heavenly Father as a bad wolf. Jesus did not come into this world to condemn it, He came to save us from death and hell, our enemies. That is Pure Love. God does not sit on this throne waiting to send lightning bolts out of heaven to strike us dead for things we have done. He waits patiently for everyone to believe in His only Begotten Son, Jesus, so you too can have eternal life. That is a blessing. The book of Revelation is a blessing, because throughout the book, you will find Jesus recorded. He is in the beginning, before the foundation of the world, and he is the end. If you have been saved, you have been blessed. I am so glad I listened to the instructions of God and kept what was written in the Bible. That was simply my faith in His Son. Even now that I'm saved, it blesses me to see others accept Christ.

If you've never been saved, you can. It is my prayer that you will. If you get saved, I'd love to hear the good news. You can email me at KLPAPLK@aol.com.

Your friend,

Kurt Klopfenstein

Author's Bio

Kurt Klopfenstein has taught Sunday school in the past, and has assisted in Vacation Bible School. He is a Missionary Baptist and enjoys spreading the gospel of Christ. He and his wife, Pamela, have three biological children; have fostered thirty-two children, and have adopted two.

www.ingramcontent.com/pod-product-compliance
Lightning Source LLC
Chambersburg PA
CBHW060632030426
42337CB00018B/3324